A leader's power

is finite,

but a leader's shared power

is infinite.

POWER EXCHANGE

How to Boost Accountability & Performance in Today's Workforce

Lee J. Colan

POWER EXCHANGE

How to Boost Accountability & Performance in Today's Workforce

Inquiries regarding permission for use of the material contained in this book should be addressed to:
CornerStone Leadership Institute
P.O. Box 764087
Dallas, TX 75376
888.789.5323

Printed in the United States of America
ISBN: 0-9772257-1-2

Credits

Design, art direction and production	Back Porch Creative, Plano, TX	info@BackPorchCreative.com
Editor	Alice Adams, Austin, TX	
Proofreader	Elizabeth Young, Dallas, TX	

TABLE OF CONTENTS

pow • er

\pou'ər\ *noun*

The ability or capacity to perform or act effectively. A specific capacity, faculty or aptitude. The ability or official capacity to exercise control; authority.

ex • change

('ĭks-chānj) *verb*

To give in return for something received. To give and receive reciprocally; interchange.

Tell me what you expect of a leader

INTRODUCTION

Consider this: Early in 2005, the workforce scale tipped once and for all. Generation X (born 1965-1977) and Generation Y (born 1978 and later) now make up the majority of the workforce. As a result, two experienced workers are leaving the workforce for every one who enters it.

Further, 10,000 Baby Boomers (born 1946-1964) turn 55 years old every day. As this workforce shift continues, so will the shift away from yesterday's workplace norms and expectations.

This new "X/Y" workforce has different expectations about work. Today's X/Y workers:

- want to know "what the deal is" – exactly what you want from them and what you have to offer them.
- have a need to be fully engaged at work to help them find a sense of meaning in their jobs and to remain satisfied.
- feel less connected to the company, and as a result, rely on their supervisors more than any other individual for information, goal clarity, policy interpretation, training, etc.
- expect their input to really matter and will leave if they see it doesn't.

Coupled with this demographic shift is the **projected shortage of more than 10 million workers in just five years**.

These new workforce dynamics and shrinking talent pool create a new leadership challenge. If this challenge is ignored it will leave leaders behind the curve of success. Those who embrace it will boost their team's competitive advantage and be the leaders of tomorrow.

The X/Y workforce will require powerful leadership. Unlike yesterday's leaders, **today's leaders *must* exchange their power for employee performance**.

A power exchange might sound counter-intuitive since power has traditionally been synonymous with leadership. However, a power exchange yields a highly energized team whether you lead any combination of full- or part-time employees, contractors, vendors, volunteers or other "free agents."

This rapid-read book presents **four simple "power converters"**– practical steps that leaders can take to boost accountability and performance. Any leader of any team at any level can use these power converters to lead today's changing workforce. The result is an advantage for your team that is sustainable and hard for competitors to replicate.

Today is the future. So, read on and exchange your power for your team's success!

"You cannot escape the responsibility of tomorrow by evading it today."

\- Abraham Lincoln

Leading with Power

A leader's power alone yields no results until it is exchanged with his team.

LEADING WITH POWER

THE POWER PARADOX

A certain level of power is inherent in any leadership position. Power typically goes to those who control information, resources and rewards.

In today's information-rich (and often time-poor) world of work, **information is the primary power source for successful leaders**.

Although leaders can certainly influence rewards and resources, these sources of power are often controlled, in large part, by the organization. However, leaders have significant control over information.

Since information is power, keeping it to ourselves can make us feel more powerful than those who do not have the information. This fundamental human dynamic has created the success of tabloid magazines. Bottom line, almost everyone wants to be in the know, even if it's just gossip.

In the X/Y workforce, the power paradox works this way: The less you control your power, the more you shift power to your team. You exchange your power – information – for team accountability and performance. Sharing your own power gives your team power.

On the other hand, the more you control your power, the less productive and engaged your team will be. Restricting the information flow with your team will choke your own success.

Let's look at how a leader of today's workforce can apply the power paradox to boost accountability and performance.

> *"It is the responsibility of leadership to provide opportunity, and the responsibility of individuals to contribute."*
>
> – William Pollard

Today's Powerful Leader

Today, nearly 85 percent of the U.S. gross domestic product comes from services and information which are created and delivered by people. People directly create the majority of value in today's economy. A leader's job is to create and sustain high levels of value *through* other people.

Today's powerful leader is willing to exchange his power to fully engage his team. He knows his employees are the fuel that powers sustained, superior performance.

The power of a leader is reflected in the power of his team. Southwest Airlines' Herb Kelleher, Jack Welch – former CEO of General Electric, Coach Phil Jackson and General Norman Schwarzkopf are considered powerful leaders. They know how to tap into the potential of their people.

Although they are leaders of mostly Baby Boomers, their leadership styles were ahead of their time. That's why they are outstanding. They don't control their power in traditional ways. Instead, they exchange their power for their team's performance. They know how to create an environment where their teams consistently give **discretionary effort – willingly going the extra mile to achieve team goals.**

Leadership Philosophy

process of exchanging power, powerful leaders also harness am's full potential by:

- creating greater personal and job challenge,
- enhancing professional growth,
- increasing employee engagement,
- building trust,
- breaking down barriers,
- raising team standards of performance and
- building employee ownership for problems and solutions.

The powerful leader, without a doubt, can still have a strong and commanding presence. The key is how he chooses to exchange information, and therefore power, to yield team success.

A power exchange is the intentional, continuous transfer of information that boosts employee accountability and performance.

Now, let's translate this definition into concrete, actionable steps called *power converters*.

"Being powerful is like being a lady.
If you have to tell people you are, you aren't."

– Margaret Thatcher

Power Converters

There are four power converters that gradually increase employee accountability and performance. These power converters give your team the biggest boost if they are applied in sequence. Since you know your team the best, you must determine when to accelerate through or spend more time on a specific power converter.

The power exchange starts by *explaining the game*. Explaining is necessary but not sufficient, in itself, to boost performance. When a leader explains something (a project, plan, expectation, process), the employee is only an observer and will likely feel little personal accountability.

The leader can continue exchanging power by *asking the right questions*. He might ask to clarify a problem or ask for ideas and suggestions. Asking questions engages employees, and as a result, they feel greater accountability.

The power exchange continues by *involving your experts* in creating solutions to improve their work and teaching them what they need to know to succeed. This step creates a high level of accountability and commitment. Employee commitment is demonstrated by identifying and solving problems and improving performance.

The final step in the power exchange is to *appreciate performance and people*. This produces a sustained level of increased accountability that results in employee ownership of their work – a new project, customer relationship, repetitive task or the quality of a report.

POWER EXCHANGE
Meter

As you progress through each power converter, you enhance your employees' responses to your leadership and elevate their level of accountability.

Let's see how a team leader, Todd, and an employee, Kristen, progress through the power converters:

Todd: "Hey, Kristen. I'm glad I bumped into you. I wanted to talk to you about something. We really need to improve our response time on special orders." (*Todd is explaining the game.*)

Kristen: "OK, I understand." (*Kristen is simply observing.*)

Todd: "You're on the front lines with this issue. Why do you think our response time has increased lately?" (*Todd is asking for input.*)

Kristen: "Well, the new system migration has had its bumps. But I think the bigger issue is that we weren't prepared for the recent promotional campaign to our VIP customers. Our call volume from VIPs has increased by 80 percent for special orders over the same period last quarter." (*Kristen is participating.*)

Todd: "We need to discuss your ideas on how we can get back on track. Our response time has a direct impact on our bottom line, so I'll give you whatever support you need to take care of this." (*Todd is involving Kristen.*)

Kristen: "That sounds great. Let me send you some initial recommendations before our meeting. I'm confident we can identify a good solution and implement it quickly." (*Now Kristen is committed to solving the problem.*)

Todd: (*After the solution is implemented*). That was a great job, Kristen. I really appreciate the way you took the initiative to explore solutions and make them happen."(*Todd is demonstrating his appreciation for Kristen and for her performance.*)

Kristen: "Thanks, Todd! It was cool to make a real difference. I've already proposed a process to the Marketing Department that will keep us in the loop and prevent this problem in the future." (*Kristen is feeling ownership of this project and of future ones!*)

Powerful leaders know **they only get accountability from their employees by being accountable to them and their success**. They understand that with today's worker, accountability is a two-way street.

Additionally, powerful leaders do not use the four power converters as separate leadership tools. Instead, they integrate the converters into their daily interactions. They also realize that using the four power converters is a time-efficient way to build **employees who act like owners and consistently give discretionary effort**.

Let's take a closer look at each of the four power converters. Each power converter has two boosters – simple actions that boost accountability and performance.

EXPLAIN THE GAME

Clarity is the friend of accountability; ambiguity is the enemy.

Leadership Philosophy

EXPLAIN THE GAME

Explaining is the most fundamental form of information exchange. It is often taken for granted with assumptions like, "I am sure they know that." or "I hired her to know that. I shouldn't have to explain it."

"Explaining the game" fills a basic need today's worker has to see the meaning or impact of their work. The challenge is that some leaders tend to fall short of explaining the game as clearly as their employees would like.

Leadership research supports this "explanation gap." A ground-breaking Harris Poll of over 11,000 households found that:

- Only 15% of workers could identify their organizations' most important goals.
- A majority of workers (51%) did not understand what they were supposed to do to help the organization achieve its goals.
- Less than half of available work time (49%) was spent on the organization's most important goals.

In light of these findings, it's easy to see how the **explanation gap can lead to an execution gap**.

In today's world of work, taking the time to provide a thorough explanation can easily take a backseat to more pressing leadership demands, firefighting and trouble shooting.

Explaining the game is a "pay me now or pay me later" leadership proposition. Try logging your firefighting tasks. How much of your time is spent on problems stemming from less-than-clear explanations of what, how and why the game is played?

To illustrate the importance of *explaining the game*, consider two sources of energy: the sun and a laser.

The sun is a powerful source of energy. It showers the earth with billions of kilowatts of energy every hour. Yet with minimal protection, say a hat and some sunscreen, you can bask in the sunlight for hours with few negative effects.

On the other hand, a laser uses a weak source of energy and *focuses* it in a cohesive stream of light, producing intense heat and power. With a laser, you can drill a hole in a diamond or defeat a cancer. That's the power of focus!

Your team's focus starts with how well you explain your vision, goals, expectations and ground rules. **A clear explanation requires less energy and yields greater results because your employees' efforts will be laser-like**. Without a clear explanation, your employees' activities will be less focused and, ultimately, less productive.

Explain the game to your team and you're on your way to winning it!

So let's discuss the two boosters that can help you *explain the game*:

- Answer the Fundamental 4
- Define the Rules of Engagement

Answer the Fundamental 4

When you explain the game, you help employees see how they fit into the big picture. People will naturally feel more accountable for their performance when they clearly understand they are a part of something bigger than themselves.

Powerful leaders explain the game by consistently answering four questions today's workers commonly ask:

1. What are we trying to achieve?
2. How are we going to achieve it?
3. How can I contribute?
4. What's in it for me?

A closer look at these four questions shows employees are really asking you to explain:

1. **Goals** – clearly defined outcomes or deliverables.
2. **Plans** – detailed, actionable steps required to achieve the goals.
3. **Roles** – broad yet clear performance expectations.
4. **Rewards** – benefits for the employee (psychologically, emotionally, intellectually and financially).

How clearly are you explaining these to your team?

Your answers to the Fundamental 4 create a bridge that connects today's possibilities to tomorrow's results. This is the bridge of accountability. Without this bridge you are dead in the water. With it, you have the necessary platform to boost your team's performance.

At the speed of today's business and information overload, it can be quite challenging to decide what to communicate to employees and what to withhold. It's easy to say (usually to ourselves), "They don't really need to know all that." or "My team won't really understand." or "I don't think they can handle that news right now." But the truth is that **leaders who *under*estimate the power of their employees generally *over*estimate their own**.

When employees don't get answers to the Fundamental 4, they tend to fill in the blanks with their own assumptions ... and their assumptions are often worst-case scenarios. This is not a reflection on the leader. It's human nature. Therefore, beware – unanswered questions start the **silence spiral**:

Silence leads to Doubt,
Doubt leads to Fear,
Fear leads to Panic,
Panic leads to Worst-Case Thinking.

This spiral can take five minutes or five weeks to develop and play out, but in most cases, it happens more rapidly than we would imagine.

Fill in the silence for your team by answering the Fundamental 4. For instance, if you learn about a new project in another department that won't affect your team for a few months, tell them about it. They can start preparing or, at minimum, they won't be caught off guard or perpetuate rumors.

Powerful leaders realize they are not protecting their teams by not informing them. They know their employees will either find out on their own or make assumptions that are often worse than reality.

The great news is that you can prevent the silence spiral ... just answer the Fundamental 4.

Define the Rules of Engagement

Rules of engagement help define how your team will interact. They are like the "We Card." signs you see in every convenience store. Those signs were created to help the store workers.

In the past, convenience store workers had to ask each customer purchasing alcohol or tobacco for identification to ensure he/she was of legal age. This became awkward for the store workers. They had to visually assess who might be close to legal age (not a position I would want to be in). As a result, they risked legal implications if they did not ask for identification from someone who was under age. They also dealt with the wrath of those who were offended by being asked for identification.

Today, with the help of "We Card." signs, workers only have to point to the sign. No fuss, no risks, nothing personal. It's a rule of engagement that is understood by all parties.

Defining the rules of engagement for your team can yield similar benefits. They create accepted ways of acting and interacting so your team does not have to think about or debate what is appropriate in each situation.

Think back to your school days. Each teacher, usually on the first day of the year, explained the classroom rules of engagement: raise your hand if you have a question, request a hall pass to use the restroom, place your homework on your desk each morning, respect others' property, etc. These rules helped both the teacher and students focus on the most important things in the classroom – learning.

Defining the rules of engagement can help your team focus on what is important – performance. They might address how to:

- make decisions,
- share information,
- consider ideas for improvement,
- coordinate hand-offs,

- review work,
- challenge prevailing thought,
- prioritize and
- resolve conflict.

Look to your team and company values for hints of appropriate rules of engagement. Your current challenges might also be a place to look for ideas. For example, one team who was having trouble getting all input on the table during their staff meetings defined these rules of engagement:

- Speak your mind during meetings, not after.
- We accept and encourage constructive disagreement as necessary to yield the best decisions for our team – nothing personal.
- We will present a unified front to the rest of the organization, regardless of disagreements during meetings.
- All problems must be presented with a solution.

Rules of engagement do not have to be wordy, but they must fit your team and be embraced by them. Here are some other examples:

- All reports must be reviewed by at least one other team member before leaving our department.
- If an issue is not resolved after five e-mails, you must meet (phone or in person) to resolve the issue.
- Customer-related tasks are always a higher priority than internal tasks.
- No team or committee meetings last more than one hour.
- Every project is debriefed for lessons learned within one week of project completion.

Today's powerful leaders keep their rules of engagement visible and apply them to decisions they make … even small decisions. These leaders also rely on their entire team to ensure each member (including themselves!) is performing within the rules of engagement. In other words, they lead and work by these rules.

Expect a few slip ups here and there, but don't worry about it! Just point to your version of the "We Card." sign – your rules of engagement.

Power Read-out

Power Converter	*Explain the Game*
Boosters	➲ Answer the Fundamental 4 ➲ Define the Rules of Engagement
Employee Accountability	Low
Employee Response	Observation

"Great leaders never tell people what to do. They set clear goals and establish the parameters. Lousy leaders think they know it all; and all the while their organization sits there, aquiver with potential."

– General Norman Schwarzkopf

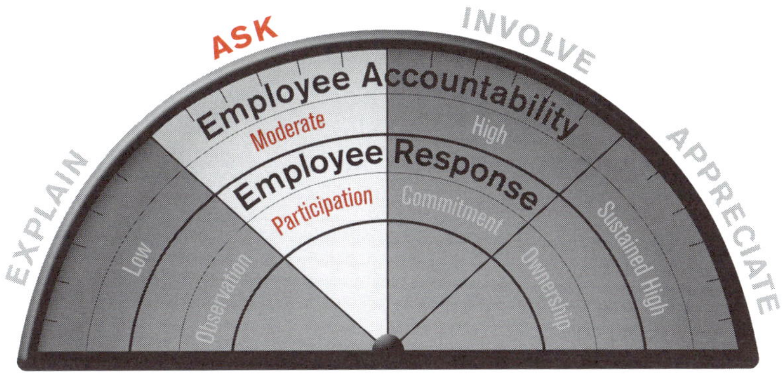

ASK THE RIGHT QUESTIONS ... THEN LISTEN

"Learn from yesterday, live for today and hope for tomorrow. The important thing is not to stop questioning."

- Albert Einstein

Ask the Right Questions ... then Listen

Explaining the game is the first step to boosting performance, but it's a one-way process. To continue your power exchange, ask the right questions. When you do, your team will be *participating* in a two-way information exchange.

Asking questions is a long-established principle to demonstrate respect, diffuse tense situations, obtain buy-in and make employees feel valued in a way that financial rewards cannot.

Understanding the two types of organizational knowledge helps underscore the importance of asking the right questions. The two types of organizational knowledge are **dashboard knowledge** and **under-the-hood knowledge**.

Dashboard knowledge is typically used by leaders. Just as your car's dashboard tells you the speed, fuel level and engine temperature, your organizational dashboard tells you if "sales are up five percent," "productivity is down" or "project deliverables are on schedule."

Under-the-hood knowledge is specific to a given job, time, place and set of circumstances. While dashboard knowledge is important for understanding general relationships and charting broad direction, it is not helpful in identifying specific actions, improvements and adjustments to help your team run more smoothly.

Under-the-hood knowledge answers why your team's engine is running hot, why it veers to the right and why it is not responding to the brake pedal as well as it should. **This is the kind of**

knowledge you can only get from people who are currently working "under the hood."

For example, Atlas Container Corporation used under-the-hood knowledge to make a critical vendor decision. Executives asked shop-floor employees to choose between competing suppliers of a $1 million machine they needed for their operation. The employees selected an American-made model, so the top executives accepted their recommendation, even though they favored a different model.

The Atlas leaders knew that under-the-hood knowledge just wouldn't show up on their dashboard. They had to ask questions to get it. They also understood the key to asking questions is to listen … really listen to the answers. **Don't ask if you won't listen**. Asking without listening only builds cynicism and drains your efforts to boost performance.

Remember what Mark Twain said: "If we were supposed to talk more than we listen, we would have two mouths and one ear." **Powerful leaders listen at least 50 percent of the time.** If you're not listening to your employees, you will gradually suffer from "blind spots" – weaknesses that are apparent to others, but not to you.

To illustrate blind spots, consider a classic episode of *Seinfeld* featuring Elaine while she was the acting president of her company. She couldn't figure out why her entire staff was suddenly shying away from her. She quickly blamed her friend George for her seeming downfall at the office. This all started to happen after a company party where Elaine, thinking she was a good dancer, did not hesitate to show off a few of her moves. Unfortunately, this was a HUGE blind spot for Elaine. It was painfully clear to everyone else that Elaine was a horrible dancer as she flailed and contorted her way across the floor!

As a viewer, you could feel the tingle of embarrassment for her and the dread if you should ever find yourself in such a situation. Fortunately for Elaine, she had an incredibly blunt friend in Kramer who, in no uncertain terms, revealed her blind spot saying, "You stink!"

Learn from Elaine. Listen to your employees, particularly your "Kramers."

Powerful leaders prevent blind spots by making concerted efforts to keep in tune with the realities of their employees – listening for the truth.

This is particularly important because **the higher you are in an organization, the more filtered the information you receive**. It's a natural and predictable phenomenon, but it's also a precarious position for any leader. No leader wants to be "Elaine on the dance floor." Therefore, the higher your leadership position, the more listening you need to do.

Ask your employees what they think, **listen to their answers** and you will be one step closer to boosting accountability and performance.

The two boosters that can help you *ask the right questions* are:

- Get the Full Story
- Think Outside the Suggestion Box

Get the Full Story

Since the information you receive can often be filtered to some degree, it's up to you to get the full story. How do you do that? Look for dissenting opinions, assumptions and perspectives to minimize your blind spots. If all you hear is "yes," be careful. The silence spiral might be spinning. In fact, don't take "yes" for a answer! **You can't wait for different opinions to come to you. Seek them out.**

Powerful leaders seek "no holds barred" input from their employees in meetings, one-on-one updates, surveys, e-mails or even in the break room.

These leaders ask their teams questions like:

- What can I do better/more of to support your success?
- What makes it hard to get your job done?
- What is the best/worst part of your job?
- If nothing was holding you back, what would you do differently?

To help you get the full story, ask *clarifying questions*. Clarifying questions will give you rich information whether you are addressing a performance problem, troubleshooting a faulty process, brainstorming ways to approach a new project or resolving an interpersonal conflict. **You will boost performance by gathering all perspectives, ideas and data before advancing your conversation or solution.**

Clarifying questions will help you transfer power to your team, prevent blind spots and boost accountability. Clarifying questions are:

- **Open-ended.** They force deeper thinking and ownership responses from employees. Close-ended questions, which require only a yes or no response, put the accountability right back on you to ask a follow-up question.

- **Specific.** An open-ended, general question is usually not very useful. Ask for specific details and data to help your team create the best solution.
- **Not imbedded with solutions.** Avoid a subtle or inferred solution or preference in your questions. Your goal is to collect information, then solutions will quickly follow.

When you ask a clarifying question, your goal is to fully understand all perspectives, assumptions and opinions so you can make the best decision for your team.

Regardless of whether or not you agree with an employee's response, understanding his response better equips you to find the best solution.

The quality of under-the-hood knowledge you gain depends not just on asking the right questions, but also on how effectively you ask them. Here are some tips from powerful leaders who really know how to get the full story:

- **Ask one question at a time.** Multiple questions usually yield an answer to only one of your questions. Wait for the response, and then ask a follow-up question.
- **Remain neutral.** Use particular caution when asking "why" questions. Your tone of voice, rolling eyes or even a sigh can infer judgment or disapproval.
- **Be patient.** Not every question has a fast answer. Your employees may need time to process an answer or even research it. Avoid temptation to interrupt or put words in the other person's mouth. Even if you are correct, you will be robbing their sense of ownership.

Asking clarifying questions is not about acquiescing to an employee's perspective. Powerful leaders are accountable for getting the full story and creating a fair and efficient decision making process (again, back to the rules of engagement).

Employees are accountable for giving you honest input about what's going on under the hood and for supporting the decision making process. Now that they are participating in the power exchange, they are closer to taking ownership for their results.

Think Outside the Suggestion Box

People are full of untapped ideas and creativity, much more than we ever capture. Unfortunately, most employees' ideas are stuck in a suggestion box … or they never even make it that far.

In addition to getting the full story, asking for ideas for improvement will boost performance. The traditional suggestion box promotes complaining, anonymity and abdication of responsibility – the exact opposites of boosting accountability and performance.

In 1992, Norman Bodek published a book featuring Toyota's idea system entitled, *40 Years, 20 Million Ideas*. It described how Toyota had reccived one million ideas per year from its employees and had been doing so for more than a decade. More recently, Toyota received more than three million ideas from employees in one year.

Several other companies have excelled at harnessing employee ideas and implementing them as a competitive advantage. Companies like Dana Corp., Milliken Corp., Yamaha, Toshiba, Technicolor Corp. and Boardroom, Inc. have each generated tens of thousands of ideas per year.

This magnitude of power exchange is *not* achieved by using a suggestion box. It *is* achieved by engaging the minds of employees and tapping into their unlimited pool of ideas and creativity. Letting this resource go untapped, as Bodek says, "It's like sitting on top of a gold mine and feeling poor."

Your first reaction to these staggering numbers of suggestions might be disbelief. How do they do it?

Before I answer that question, let's address why we should even focus on asking for ideas when we are trying to boost performance. This booster is not about ideas for ideas' sake. It is about soliciting ideas to improve employee productivity, reduce costs, increase speed and eliminate waste. The primary objective is to improve individual and team performance.

The by-product of this booster is a strong and rapid increase in the employees' sense of accountability. These under-the-hood ideas will ultimately make their work more interesting, efficient and challenging. Your team will realize cost savings, quality and service improvements, as well as an irreplaceable competitive advantage.

Okay, back to the question: How do they do it? **The name of the game is to think small.** Small ideas are actually better than big ideas because small ideas:

- are **much more likely to stay proprietary** and create sustainable competitive advantage since they are situation-specific. Besides, your competitors are most likely looking for the next big idea. Let them wait for their grand slam while you hit a thousand singles.
- enable you to **focus on the details of your business**.

Excellence is a result of getting the details right. In many cases, it is literally impossible to improve performance (speed, service, quality, costs) beyond a certain level without small ideas.

- help **create a culture that values ideas** (every idea is a good idea) and the people they come from, resulting in a boost in ownership at the grassroots level of your organization.
- facilitate **rapid and continuous organizational learning** and performance improvements based on that learning.
- are the **best sources of big ideas** (the *Post-it* note came from a small idea to find a better glue).

Small ideas might include: "If we eliminated the cover page on internal faxes, we would save 150 pieces of paper per month," "While I am waiting for our driver to check in his shipment at our store's receiving dock, I sweep out his truck so he can make a quicker turnaround at our distribution center" or "If I highlight off-plan line items on my report, the executive committee can more quickly and efficiently focus on those areas of concern."

Powerful leaders go for quantity of ideas, not quality. They make ideas, lots of them, part of everyone's job. They use clarifying questions to determine if and how to best implement the ideas.

Ask your team for the kinds of ideas you need. You may have a focal area for that week, month or quarter. A good place to start is with the **eight areas of waste**. These are the enemies of profit:

- Defects (incorrect/incomplete information, rework)
- Inventory (batching, excess orders in process)
- Processing (unnecessary steps, unneeded precision)
- Waiting (materials, information, tools not ready)

- ➲ Motion (choosing, searching, retrieving, storing)
- ➲ Transportation (mailing, faxing, traveling, walking)
- ➲ Overproduction (working ahead, outpacing next process)
- ➲ Underutilized talent (the worst one of all!)

Make ideas the currency you exchange for employee accountability and your return on investment will be amazing!

"Good ideas are common – what's uncommon are people who'll work hard enough to bring them about."

– Ashleigh Brilliant

Power Read-out

Power Converter	*Ask the Right Questions … then Listen*
Boosters	➲ Get the Full Story ➲ Think Outside the Suggestion Box
Employee Accountability	Moderate
Employee Response	Participation

INVOLVE
YOUR EXPERTS

"Few things can help an individual more than to place responsibility on him, and to let him know that you trust him."
– Booker T. Washington

INVOLVE YOUR EXPERTS

By asking your employees questions, you encourage them to participate in a two-way information exchange. To continue your power exchange, involve employees in improving their jobs and your business. Take the ideas they give you and involve them in developing solutions to problems, identifying areas for improvement and finding opportunities for growth.

Involve the people who are under the hood, your experts, in seeking new ways to reduce expenses, expedite customer service or improve coordination with other departments. Employees will exchange their involvement for high accountability and commitment to the desired results.

People support what they help create. By involving employees, you challenge them to be accountable for tackling new issues and solving problems. Require team members to bring you solutions along with problems. There is no hiding from problems when accountability prevails.

Even the most powerful leaders sometimes feel threatened by the idea of involving their employees in identifying and solving problems. Perhaps they feel they're giving up control over *how* their team will achieve its goals.

However, powerful leaders also realize there is more than one way to effectively solve a problem. An employee's approach might be different than the leaders, but the benefits of building ownership that come from employees creating the solutions far outweigh any loss of control powerful leaders might feel.

When employees are involved, the buck doesn't stop with the leader – it stops with each employee on the team. Consider the following conversation between two employees:

> **Joe:** "Boy, I sure would like to ask the boss why he let things get so out of control with our team. Seems like we're being really inefficient, we're not sure what to do and no one is having much fun."
>
> **Lynn:** "Yea, I'd like to hear his answer too. So what's stopping you from asking him?"
>
> **Joe:** "Oh, uh, well … I'm afraid he might ask me the same question!"

This conversation will not occur on a team whose leader applies these two boosters to *involve your experts*:

- Streamline Success
- Teach to Learn

It's not who is right, it's what is right that matters.

STREAMLINE SUCCESS

Sometimes the process of involving team members to achieve success has the unintended consequence of preventing success. Like most attempts to use a suggestion box, the stepping stones to success can become stumbling blocks of bureaucracy. Your goal is to convert ideas into action and exchange involvement for results.

To achieve this, **streamline success by giving your team authority to suggest *and* implement ideas**. This builds a culture of accountability … no excuses here.

Let's look at Toyota again. Each year, Toyota's employees implement more than one million ideas that save the company over $300 million annually. Virtually all of these ideas are implemented at the employee level. Even though many of Toyota's employees perform repetitive jobs, they are fully involved and engaged in improving their work output and their work lives.

Problems and improvements are identified, solved and measured by each team – the experts in their jobs. It's not the company mandating these improvements; rather accountability and results are driven at the frontline team level, where the rubber meets the road.

It's no surprise that Toyota is expected to surpass DaimlerChrysler as one of the "Big Three" automakers in America. This unprecedented market share gain is powered by a culture of ideas and accountability.

Inspired by Toyota's success, a decade ago, the Chairman and CEO of Dana Corporation asked his 80,000 employees to submit two creative ideas per month and implement 80 percent of them. For more than 10 years Dana's employees implemented about two million ideas per year, saving over $2 billion.

And this idea keeps on working. In 2003, Subaru averaged 108 ideas per employee which resulted in savings of $39 million. This equated to savings of $5,000 per employee.

These amazing results required no executive approval or committees. Now that's streamlining success!

What kind of impact would this have in your team?

Leading organizations that exchange power for performance apply these **principles to streamline success**:

- Ideas are part of everyone's job.
- It's easy to submit ideas.
- Ideas are reviewed by people with under-the-hood knowledge, who will be directly affected if the ideas are implemented.
- Decisions on each idea are made quickly and effectively.
- Feedback to the employee suggesting the idea is quick and complete. In most cases, they should be involved in the decision so feedback is instantaneous.
- Whenever possible, and in most cases, ideas are implemented immediately.
- The process for managing ideas, as informal as it may be, is always monitored and improved.

These simple principles force us to realize just how small and manageable each idea must be to sustain such an informal, efficient decision making process.

The *Idea Tracker* form on the next page reflects the elegant simplicity and efficiency that enables a power exchange.

Avoid approaching this like just another program or you might end up trapped inside the suggestion box. Take it slow – this may be a fundamental shift for your team.

Start by setting an idea goal for your employees – let's say one small idea per month. Use early wins to reinforce the merits of streamlining success, build momentum and spread enthusiasm.

You are dealing with small ideas, so take small steps. Streamline success and it will be a big idea and a big step ahead of your competition!

Complexity creates a maze between you and success.
Simplicity ensures a clear line of sight.

My Team's Idea Tracker

Suggester	Idea	Priority	Implementer
Donna	Put yellow tape on the first step into the mailroom to prevent people from tripping on the step.	High	Donna
Jay	Pack a preset portable box with meeting supplies that can be easily taken to off-site meetings to avoid paying hotel fees for these items. We spent $1,500 to rent these items last year.	High	Jay
Rose	Set up incoming faxes to arrive into the Admin's PC in each department to save paper. Only print if needed. We average 100 faxes/month at 3 pgs. each. Admin says she only needs to print half of them. This saves us 50 pgs./month plus less printer wear and tear.	Medium	Pete
Bill	Post our chart of account codes on our intranet so managers can correctly code invoices and reduce the number of late payments to key vendors. Currently 50% of our invoices must be returned or corrected, each taking an average of 3 additional days to process.	High	Jay
Pete	Two back doors to warehouse are often left open. Install simple spring-loaded door hinges to keep them closed for safety and to save on A/C bill.	Low	Pete

Teach to Learn

Powerful leaders boost accountability and performance by teaching … and learning. As the proverb states, “In teaching others, we teach ourselves.” So teach your team in order to boost your own learning.

Did you know the average person possesses between 500 and 700 different skills and abilities? Teach your team key skills including: alertness, data collection, problem identification, problem solving and communication.

Let’s focus on the skill of *alertness* because it’s critical for generating lots of under-the-hood ideas.

When people become aware of something – a problem, an area for cutting cost, a pattern of reactions – they tend to see more of that thing. This can be called the *yellow car phenomenon.*

When was the last time you saw a yellow car? You might see a yellow car once a day or so. Now, for the next week check out how many yellow cars you see.

Since I have alerted you to yellow cars, you will probably observe many more of them than you had previously noticed. Is it because so many more yellow cars just hit the streets? Of course not. You just sharpened your alertness.

Sharpen your team’s alertness by encouraging them to: pay attention to exceptions, write down their thoughts and observations, and spend time studying problems.

Another way to sharpen alertness is to expose your people to new experiences to broaden their perspectives and deepen their knowledge, including:

- job rotation,
- reading groups,
- professional associations,
- cross-functional teams,
- industry benchmarking,
- presentations to management and
- training colleagues (the best test of learning is to be able to teach someone else).

Although all of these are great teaching tools, don't forget about the most important source of learning for your employees – YOU!

Share your experiences. There are lessons to be found in everything your team does. Look for opportunities in post-project reviews, customer meetings, conflicts with other departments, changes in priorities, miscommunications and mistakes. Seize all these experiences to teach your team … and learn from them.

A simple, yet powerful, teaching tool is called, the *five whys*. This tool facilitates team learning through discovery. Use it when your team is trying to identify the root cause of a problem or determine cause-effect relationships for certain aspects of your operation.

For example, let's say your team is brainstorming the root cause of consistently missing their month-end close deadline. The *five whys* might unfold like this:

Why do we keep missing our month-end close deadline?
– Because our invoices are backlogged.

Why are our invoices backlogged?
– Because we receive a large number of them from the field on the last two days of the month.

Why do we receive so many of them during the last two days?
– Because most of the invoices are awaiting approval by managers at corporate.

Why are our corporate managers waiting to approve the invoices?
– Because they are waiting for us to give them the chart of account codes to assign to the invoice.

Why are they waiting for the codes from us?
– Because we forgot to post our chart of accounts on the company intranet earlier this year.

As you can see the *five whys* can help you quickly get to the core of an issue and take a good look under the hood.

This tool is particularly useful for cutting through excuses and boosting accountability. However, don't get caught in the trap of using this exercise to assign blame. Use it, instead, to focus on the learnings and solutions you will discover together.

Powerful leaders are great teachers; great teachers are great learners. So teach to learn and boost your team's performance.

POWER READ-OUT

Power Converter	*Involve Your Experts*
Boosters	➲ Streamline Success ➲ Teach to Learn
Employee Accountability	High
Employee Response	Commitment

"You learn something every day if you pay attention."

– Ray LeBlond

APPRECIATE
PERFORMANCE AND PEOPLE

People will forget what you said.
People will even forget what you did.
But people will never forget how you made them feel.

APPRECIATE PERFORMANCE AND PEOPLE

William James, the father of psychology, stated that a fundamental human need is to be appreciated. This idea is supported by many studies that show the number one need expressed by employees is *to feel fully appreciated for their work*. The bottom line: **We do more for those who appreciate us.**

Appreciating employees and recognizing their contributions completes the power exchange from you to your employees. Your appreciation will be converted into *sustained* high accountability because people want to do more and do it better when they know they are appreciated. Employees will respond by acting like owners of your business. Here's where you will see a real surge in employees' discretionary effort!

Although leaders widely recognize the need for employee appreciation, it tends to be a blind spot. **Leaders generally believe they are much more appreciative of their employees than their employees think they are**.

In fact, this blind spot was clearly revealed in a study comparing how 10,000 employees ranked 10 work-related values against how their managers *thought* their employees would rank these values.

The employees' top two rankings were: full appreciation for work done and feeling in on things. On the other hand, managers thought employees would rank these two values eighth and tenth, respectively – that's nearly the exact opposite of what their employees thought – a big blind spot.

We might hear ourselves say, "Gee, I meant to tell Ron what a great job he did." or "Well, I intended to acknowledge Jackie for stepping outside her comfort zone on that last project." **We tend to judge ourselves by our intentions, but others judge us by our actions.**

That's why there is a gap between our own perceptions (our intentions) and our employees' perceptions of our appreciativeness (our actions). Showing appreciation for our teams is not a matter of time and intention. It's a matter of priority and action.

The two boosters that will help you *appreciate performance and people* are:

- Create Defining Moments
- Know Your People, Not Just Your Employees

"An automobile goes nowhere efficiently unless it has a quick, hot spark to ignite things, to set the cogs in motion. So I try to make every player on my team feel like he's the spark keeping our machine in motion. On him depends our successes."

– Knute Rockne

Create Defining Moments

According to Nobel Prize winning scientist Daniel Kahneman, we experience approximately 20,000 individual moments in a waking day. Each "moment" lasts a few seconds. If you consider your strongest memories, positive or negative, you'll notice the imagery in your mind is actually defined by your recollection of a precise point in time.

In some cases, a single encounter can change your life forever. Think of your own defining moments. Are they literally moments?

Your role as a leader is incredibly powerful. You have the opportunity to create defining moments for your employees *every day*.

Demonstrating your appreciation for your employees and their efforts can put them on the fast track to ownership behavior. There should be plenty of opportunities since a Harris Poll found that 65 percent of the workers reported receiving ***no recognition*** for good work in the past year!

Look for moments to acknowledge your team's efforts and results. This is basic psychology – reinforce those behaviors that you want to see more frequently. Catch them doing something right … and do it often.

Research by the former chairman of Gallup, Donald Clifton, revealed **workgroups with at least a 3-to-1 ratio of positive to negative interactions were significantly more productive than those having less than a 3-to-1 ratio**. (The same study showed the key ratio for marriages was 5-to-1.) What is the ratio for your team? Is it 1:1, 3:1, 5:1 or 10:1?

Consider tracking your team's ratio for a week to gauge how well you are appreciating your employees. Don't worry about showing too much appreciation. To date, there are no documented cases of employees, or anyone else for that matter, feeling *over*-appreciated!

The good news is that you have complete control over this type of appreciation. No budget limitations or excuses here – there are literally thousands of ways to create defining moments. Here are a few:

- Say "Thank You!" – an all-too-obvious yet highly underused form of appreciation.
- Allow employees to present their work to *your* boss. This is a great way to engage employees, and it also shows your boss what kind of leader you are.
- Offer team members a choice of projects to work on. When employees buy into a project, they will put their hearts into it.
- Put a sincere acknowledgement in your company or department newsletter. This takes only a few minutes of your time, but creates long-term "trophy value" for the employee.
- Tell an employee's story of accomplishment at a staff meeting. Stories are perceived as more interesting, meaningful, thoughtful and memorable.
- Take a team member to lunch to show your appreciation. Remember to do more listening than talking.

These and other expressions of appreciation solidify all of the work you did in the prior three power converters.

g moments also become key stories that comprise your biography – these moments create a rich folklore that is passed on and reinforces your team's culture of accountability and performance.

> *"Life is not measured by the number of breaths we take, but by the moments that take our breath away."*
>
> – George Carlin

Know Your People, Not Just Your Employees

After interviewing 25,000 leaders, Ferdinand Fournies found the most effective ones had one thing in common – they expressed a sincere interest in their employees. "Sincere" is the operative word here. Your motivation matters! If you appreciate employees in hopes of getting something in return, they will see right through you.

Appreciate your people, not just their contributions. Learn something new each day about one of your employees. Ask them about their families, hobbies, leisure activities, etc. Then weave this information into your interactions with them. They will return your appreciation with discretionary effort.

After an extensive three-year study of the critical variables for leadership success, the Center for Creative Leadership concluded that the only statistically significant factor differentiating the very best leaders from mediocre ones is caring. **People don't care how much you know until they know how much you care.** This particularly holds true for employees and their leaders.

Show your team you care by staying plugged in to them. Today's technology offers many options – Blackberries, pagers, cell phone text messages, instant messaging, voice mail, e-mail. Be cautious of overuse of these communication options – they might cause a power outage instead of a power exchange.

With all of these technology options, it's easy to find ourselves too busy for face-to-face interaction, but that's one of the best ways to charge up our teams. **We work in a high-tech world, but leadership is still a high-touch job**.

Regardless of which channels you use to exchange information with your team, being accessible to them is the key to staying plugged in. Demonstrating that you are available to help your team be successful is quickly exchanged for discretionary effort.

You know best what makes your employees tick. Appreciation is certainly not a one-size-fits-all need. It should to be customized to each employee, so **personalize your recognition**.

For example, being recognized at an all-employee meeting might trigger more perspiration than inspiration for an introverted employee. Instead, use the information you learn about your employees to present an appropriate gift, token or sincere expression of appreciation. Invariably, the gift will be less important than the obvious time and thoughtfulness that went into it.

Know your people, not just your employees. You will begin to understand them more fully and then be able to more effectively express your appreciation … and boost performance!

Power Read-out

Power Converter	*Appreciate Performance and People*
Boosters	➲ Create Defining Moments ➲ Know Your People, Not Just Your Employees
Employee Accountability	Sustained High
Employee Response	Ownership

"Everyone has an invisible sign hanging from their neck saying, 'Make me feel important.' Never forget this message when working with people."

– Mary Kay Ash

POWERING UP!

"Success on any major scale requires you to accept responsibility ... in the final analysis, the one quality that all successful people have ... is the ability to take on responsibility."

– Michael Korda

Power Converters	Boosters	Employee Accountability	Employee Response
Explain the Game	➲ Answer the Fundamental 4 ➲ Define the Rules of Engagement	Low	Observation
Ask the Right Questions … then Listen	➲ Get the Full Story ➲ Think Outside the Suggestion Box	Moderate	Participation
Involve Your Experts	➲ Streamline Success ➲ Teach to Learn	High	Commitment
Appreciate Performance and People	➲ Create Defining Moments ➲ Know Your People, Not Just Your Employees	Sustained High	Ownership

"I am only one, but still I am one. I cannot do everything, but still I can do something; And because I cannot do everything I will not refuse to do the something that I can do."

– Edward Everett Hale

POWERING UP!

Your leadership sets the limits of your team's accountability and performance. Integrate the four power converters into your leadership repertoire and your team will deliver heroic efforts and unbeatable results!

Take the complimentary *Power Exchange* Calibrator to see how well you are applying the four power converters. Based on your score, you will receive an action plan to help you boost your team's accountability and performance.

You can find the *Power Exchange* Calibrator at www.theLgroup.com.

EXPERIENCING THE POWER

Nordstrom is a retailer that is internationally known for delivering superior customer service because their people take personal ownership for satisfying each shopper's individual needs.

A couple of years ago, a friend of mine was in Nordstrom, shopping for a gift – a certain perfume. This brand of perfume had long been his wife's favorite and he knew Nordstrom would have a good selection.

But when he reached the fragrance counter, he was surprised to find that Nordstrom didn't carry that particular perfume. "I'm sorry, sir," apologized the associate. "We haven't carried that fragrance for some time. However, if you have about 15 minutes, I'll see what I can do."

Agreeing to return in 15 minutes, he browsed through other departments to see if something else caught his eye. Fifteen minutes later, he returned to the fragrance counter and there was the associate with the perfume he was seeking in hand asking if he would like to have it gift wrapped.

"But ... how? Where did you find it?" he asked, thinking it may have been found in some dark corner of a back room.

"One of the stores here in the mall carries it, so I ran down and bought it right away," the associate responded.

"But how did you pay for it?" my friend wanted to know.

"I used my own money," she replied.

"So, tell me, how much do I owe you?" he asked.

She told him the amount, gift wrapped the precious bottle of perfume, smiled and my friend was on his way, relieved to have found what he was looking for.

As my friend relayed the story to me, I marveled at an organization that was able to instill such pride of ownership into each employee, so I began researching Nordstrom's leadership approach.

What I found was that Nordstrom has flipped the typical organizational pyramid, so customers are at the top of the chart, the top priority, followed by sales associates and other support staff. At the bottom are the CEO and other company officials. That's a literal power exchange!

Nordstrom's power exchange boosts their sales associate accountability and ownership. As a result, Nordstrom's stellar customer service has become the gold standard in retailing and serves as a benchmark for other industries.

THE POWER SOURCE

You are the power source for your team. How you distribute your power is your choice.

Powering up your team is like charging a battery. It takes time for the power to be gradually transferred from the power source (the leader) to the battery (your team).

Once fully powered, the battery can generate strong voltage (performance) for awhile, but not forever. To sustain higher performance levels, the power converters must be used continuously to recharge your team and sustain the output you want.

As you incorporate power exchange into your leadership style, you will begin to see remarkable results. As the voltage rises, so will your team's performance level.

Ultimately, your power exchange, like the power exchange that has fueled excellence at Toyota, Nordstrom and other industry leaders, will boost your team past the competition!

Power horded yields destruction.
Power exchanged yields production.

Six ways to reinforce *Power Exchange*

1. Keynote Presentation

Invite author Lee J. Colan to power up your team and share insights to help you fuel your power exchange.

2. Workshop

Facilitated by the author or a certified facilitator, this three- or six-hour workshop will reinforce the principles of *Power Exchange* and guide participants through the power exchange process using relevant examples so they can get started right away. Participants will create personal plans to boost their team's performance.

3. PowerPoint® Presentation

Introduce and reinforce the "power converters" to your team with this professionally designed presentation. Use the presentation for staff meetings, brown bag lunches or as a follow-up development tool. $99.95

4. At-a-Glance Reminder Cards

These attractively designed, quick-reference cards summarize the four power converters for boosting your team's performance. Perfect for every leader to have at their fingertips! 5" x 7" cards. Pk/10 $19.95

5. "What's the Small Idea?" Pads

A great tool to generate lots of ideas and streamline success. Give one of these handy pads to every employee to submit ideas for improvement. 9" x 6" pads, 50 pgs/pad. Pk/5 $14.95

6. *Power Exchange* Calibrator

Take this free, online *Power Exchange* Calibrator based one the four power converters revealed in this book. A five-minute investment will yield a personalized plan to help you boost your team's accountability and performance! Go to www.theLgroup.com. Complimentary

Leader's Performance Package

Sticking to It: The Art of Adherence by Lee J. Colan reveals the secrets to success for high-achieving individuals and teams. It offers practical steps to help you consistently execute your plans. Read it and WIN! $9.95

Passionate Performance: Engaging Minds and Hearts to Conquer the Competition by Lee J. Colan, offers practical strategies to engage the minds and hearts of your team at home, work, church or in the community. Read it and conquer your competition! $9.95

Orchestrating Attitude by Lee J. Colan translates the incomprehensible into the actionable. It cuts through the clutter to deliver inspiration and application so you can orchestrate your attitude … and your success! $9.95

Monday Morning Leadership is David Cottrell's best-selling book. It offers unique encouragement and direction that will help you become a better manager, employee and person. $14.95
Monday Morning Leadership Audio CD $19.95

Management Insights explores the myths and realities of management. It provides insight into how you can become a successful manager. $14.95

The Manager's Communication Handbook is a powerful handbook that helps you connect with employees and create the understanding, support and acceptance critical to your success. $9.95

The Manager's Coaching Handbook is a practical guide to improving performance from your superstars, middle stars and falling stars. $9.95

175 Ways to Get More Done in Less Time has 175 excellent tips and techniques to help you get things done faster … and better. $9.95

Becoming the Obvious Choice is a roadmap showing employees how they can maintain their motivation, develop their hidden talents and become their best. $9.95

136 Effective Presentation Tips is a powerful handbook providing 136 practical, easy-to-use tips to make every presentation a success. $9.95

Listen Up, Leader! Ever wonder what employees think about their leaders? This book tells you the seven characteristics of leadership that people will follow. $9.95

Order Form

1-99 copies $9.95 100-499 copies $8.95 500+ copies $7.95

Power Exchange ____ copies X ______ = $______

Power Exchange Companion Resources

PowerPoint® Presentation (downloadable)	____ copies X $99.95	= $______
At-a-Glance Reminder Cards (pk/10)	____ pack(s) X $19.95	= $______
"What's the Small Idea?" Pads (pk/5)	____ pack(s) X $14.95	= $______

Additional Leadership Development Resources

The ULTIMATE ADVANTAGE Series (Includes *Sticking to It, Passionate Performance & Orchestrating Attitude)*	____ set(s) X $27.95	= $______
Leader's Performance Package (Includes all products listed on previous page)	____ pack(s) X $129.95	= $______

Other Books

______________________	____ copies X ______	= $______
______________________	____ copies X ______	= $______
______________________	____ copies X ______	= $______
	Shipping & Handling	$______
	Subtotal	$______
	Sales Tax (8.25%-TX Only)	$______
	Total (U.S. Dollars Only)	**$**______

Shipping and Handling Charges

Total $ Amount	Up to $50	$51-$99	$100-$249	$250-$1199	$1200-$2999	$3000+
Charge	$6	$9	$16	$30	$80	$125

Name ______________________ Job Title ______________

Organization ______________________ Phone ______________

Shipping Address ______________________ Fax ______________

Billing Address ______________________ **Email** ______________
(required when ordering PowerPoint® Presentation)

City ______________________ State __________ ZIP __________

❑ Please invoice (Orders over $200) Purchase Order Number (if applicable) ______________

Charge Your Order: ❑ MasterCard ❑ Visa ❑ American Express

Credit Card Number ______________________ Exp. Date __________

Signature ______________________________________

❑ Check Enclosed (Payable to: CornerStone Leadership)

Phone 888.789.5323
Fax 972.274.2884

www.**CornerStoneLeadership**.com

Mail
P.O. Box 764087
Dallas, TX 75376

CornerStone

Leadership Institute

www.CornerStoneLeadership.com